Cremation Today and Tomorrow

Gorgias Liturgical Studies

19

This series is intended to provide a venue for studies about liturgies as well as books containing various liturgies. Making liturgical studies available to those who wish to learn more about their own worship and practice or about the traditions of other religious groups, this series includes works on service music, the daily offices, services for special occasions, and the sacraments.

Cremation Today and Tomorrow

J. Douglas Davies

gorgias press

2010

Gorgias Press LLC, 180 Centennial Ave., Piscataway, NJ, 08854, USA

www.gorgiaspress.com

2010　　　ϰ

ISBN 978-1-60724-370-0　　　　　　　**ISSN 1937-3252**

Published first in the U.K. by Grove Books, 1990.

Printed in the United States of America

Cremation Today and Tomorrow

by J. Douglas Davies

Senior Lecturer in Theology, University of Nottingham
Director, Cremation Research Project

CONTENTS

Preface

Cremation is now so widespread in Britain that a short study is called for as a means of stimulating discussion among professionals and interested parties at large. It is an area requiring research to guarantee that issues are taken beyond the local level and further than story and anecdote. This at least is what I have attempted in the following pages and with the help of material from two major research projects. Very much more material exists than is mentioned here and this will be analyzed and published in due course.

The Cremation Research Project of which I am the Director was funded by a Nottingham University Research Award provided by the Nottinghamshire County Council and I would thank both parties for their help. Mr. Matthew Carter, a geography graduate, served as my research assistant on this project and did much work on questionnaire analysis and interviewing. I take this opportunity to thank him for his thoroughness and amiability.

On The Rural Church Project I am a Co-Director along with Dr. Michael Winter and Dr. Charles Watkins, both of the Royal Agricultural College, Cirencester. Funded by the Leverhulme Trust and by the Archbishops' Commission on Rural Affairs, this was an extensive study of clergy and people in the dioceses of Durham, Lincoln, Southwell, Gloucester, and Truro. Research Assistants on this project included Mr. Christopher Short from Cirencester, who has been particularly helpful over cremation material.

I would like to thank the clergy of Southwell Diocese for their patience in answering additional questionnaires on cremation, and hundreds of people in Nottinghamshire for doing the same. Many Directors of British Crematoria and officers of both the Cremation Society of Great Britain, and the Federation of British Cremation Authorities have been of great help in many ways and I thank them all. Let me also thank Bishop Colin Buchanan and the Rev. Michael Vasey for encouragement, and finally Mr. Matthew Falkiner of Nottingham University's Architecture Department for the cover design.

Introduction

Nearly three quarters of all Britons are cremated. In terms of other historically Christian cultures this is an extraordinary high figure. In 1988, for example, approximately 70% of British cremations compared with 15% in the U.S.A., 31% in Canada, 43% in Holland and 57% in Switzerland. Strictly Catholic countries show a very low rate of cremation as in the case of Italy's 1% and Spain's 11%, (*Pharos* 1989: Vol. 5. No.4).

This dramatic shift from burial to cremation, especially since 1945, marks a major social and liturgical change in customary behaviour. After an initial period of theological opposition to cremation most churches have become deeply involved in it, but they have paid relatively little formal attention to theological issues involved. Clergy conduct the great majority of the half million or so cremations performed each year in the United Kingdom but the rites they perform still assume underlying ideas derived from the traditional funeral service of burial.

Now that cremation has claimed centre stage in British funeral practice the time is right to rethink liturgical, pastoral, and theological issues of this major feature of the church's ministry as it touches the great proportion of the general public. This is one area where liturgical practice and pastoral theology invite a discussion of a more doctrinal and systematic nature. The key issues I want to raise involve:

1. Resurrection and Eternal Life
   What do people believe about life after death? Is the astonishing speed at which cremation has come to be the dominant form of funerary rite in Britain associated with an equally speedy decline in belief in an after-life?
2. Pastoral Practice and Cultural Life
   Are changes in patterns of belief likely to lead to fewer people wanting the services of clergy as officiants at funerals?
3. The Body, Cremation, and the Church
   What is the human body in relation to theological thought and in the life shared by people and ended by death?
4. Clerical and Lay Views
   How do clergy and people's views of cremation relate to each other?
5. Theology of Cremation
   Is it possible to have a theology of cremation?
6. Cremation as a Christian Rite
   If a theology of cremation is possible how might it influence the form of cremation rites

In analyzing these issues I have set myself three tasks. Firstly to present data from my own research on cremation and religious belief. Secondly to offer some theological ideas on cremation derived from a dual commitment both to pastoral theology and social anthropology. Thirdly to produce a specimen cremation service which is both Christian and culturally appropriate.

Individuals demand respect, especially over issues which they seldom discuss yet feel deeply. In the research lying behind this book we have sought to listen before speaking and to make both theology and liturgy a feedback between scripture, tradition, and the experience of both clergy and ordinary men and women. Sadly very little material exists to enable me to talk about children who are often ignored in bereavement.

In the Alternative Service Book the additional rites of a funeral of a child, prayers at interment of ashes, a service for use before a funeral and for a still-birth all very properly indicate pastoral concern. What is theologically interesting, however, is that little attempt was made to differentiate between burial and cremation. Although burial continues to provide the root metaphor for cremation many people find that this image contradicts their experience of cremation. To rethink cremation is to develop traditional liturgical and pastoral concern by means of theological analysis related to historical aspects of social change.

THE MODERN HISTORY OF CREMATION

Although there was some discussion of cremation in the seventeenth century it was the late nineteenth century that marked the birth of modern cremation in Britain. It was in no sense a theological or church based movement. On the contrary freethought and liberal attitudes typified the values surrounding this desire for apparently healthier and environmentally safer forms of disposing of the dead,(Leaney 1989:124).

A model crematorium at the Vienna Exposition of 1873 caught the attention of Sir Henry Thompson, surgeon to Queen Victoria. He wrote on the subject and invited various people to join him in promoting the idea of cremation. This initiative gave birth to the Cremation Society of England in 1874, but it was to be another ten years before a judicial pronouncement asserted the legality of cremation.

This case concerned the eccentric Dr.William Price of Llantrisant in South Wales. He claimed to be a Druidic high priest, named his baby son Jesus Christ, and, when the child died an infant, Dr. Price tried cremating him, only to be stopped in the process by a crowd regarding the act as pagan, (Islwyn ap Nicholas 1973). The case, heard in Cardiff in February 1884, is interesting in that the judge presented a detailed history of funerary rites prior to his decision that cremation was not a criminal offence as long as it caused no public nuisance, (*Law Reports* Vol. XII, 1884, 12 QB 247). In philosophical terms the judge was largely concerned with the issue of speed. Cremation did quickly what burial did slowly. The actual destruction of the corpse was, he thought, something horrible which healthy imaginations turned away from, and which funerary procedures should conceal from observation.

This legal decision opened the way for cremation as a normal means of disposing of the dead. But the very phrase 'disposing of the dead', along with the fact that it was a legal decision that had sanctioned the new development, made the religious status of this procedure somewhat ambivalent. Was cremation like burial? The fact that early proponents of cremation suggested that burned remains should either be retained in urns or buried hinted at the partial or ambiguous nature of cremation, and of what might best be called 'memorial remains'. In other words cremation was not the end of the matter when it came to human bodies.

In earlier Christian periods and until the earlier nineteenth century burial did not involve coffins. Public graves might contain shrouded bodies or closely packed coffins. In the nineteenth century there was even an 'Earth to Earth Society' which sought to banish durable coffins to allow the earth to accept and purify dead bodies, (Morley,1971:96). With modern burial there is a high degree of certainty as far as memory and memorials are concerned. The coffin is buried in a specific place and left there. It is a single event. With cremation the main event is the destruction of the body by fire, but then there are ashes to dispose of in some way or other. The very fact of choice over this makes for a degree of uncertainty.

In Britain in 1986 the Federation of British Cremation Authorities reported that cremated remains were handled as shown in this table:

Table 1 Location of Cremated Remains 1986
57% Strewn in Grounds
15% Interred in Grounds
4% Placed in graves or niches
22% Taken away by representatives
2% Retained pending instructions

(Federation of British Cremation Authorities Report 1986)

It is likely that a high proportion of those taken by families were subsequently buried or disposed of in some way chosen according to the will of the deceased. There are no nation wide facts available on this point, the limited information available from the Cremation Research Project suggests that perhaps only some 4% of individuals wish to have idiosyncratic placing of their own ashes.

Historically speaking cremation in Britain officially began at the Woking crematorium in 1885 with three bodies. The following year witnessed ten cremations, while 1888 marked twenty eight. Cremation companies and societies then began to emerge in other parts of the country: Manchester in 1892, Glasgow in 1895 and the famous Golders Green Crematorium at the turn of the century. In 1902 an Act of Parliament formally recognized cremation as a means of disposing of the dead and in 1903 rules for the proper cremation of human remains were published by the Home Secretary.

CHURCHES AND CREMATION
As far as the churches were concerned support for cremation was divided. The Dean and Chapter of St.Paul's Cathedral decided in 1910 that cremation was a prerequisite for any person who was to be 'buried' in the Cathedral. The Birmingham Crematorium of 1903 was built with the permission of the bishops of Worcester, Lichfield, and Coventry. In 1922 and 1923 the bishops of Lincoln, and St. Edmondsbury were cremated while in 1944 William Temple as Archbishop of Canterbury was cremated.

It is of some interest to see that when Charles Forder wrote his widely used manual, *The Parish Priest at Work*, in 1947 he not only generally commended the practice but mentioned William Temple's cremation as evidence in support of it. The Roman Catholic Church took longer to arrive at its present position. Catholics were permitted cremation in 1963 but a further three years' wait was required before priests were allowed to perform cremation ceremonies in crematoria. So it was not until the mid nineteen-sixties that all the major churches in England and Wales agreed on the acceptability of cremation.

But this is to ignore the Greek Orthodox tradition, which still deems cremation an improper means of treating that body which is the basis of the resurrection body, a reality which in Orthodox tradition shares so immediately in the central resurrection body of Christ. From a quite different end of the theological and liturgical spectrum the Free Presbyterian Church in Scotland has opposed the building of a Crematorium in Inverness in the Spring of 1990. One of their ministers is reported to have said that biblical authority supported burial and that it was a decline in biblical standards that had accompanied the rise of cremation in Britain. So the theological question cannot simply be taken as settled.

The earliest Christian tradition itself favoured burial to the extent that cremation disappeared by the fourth and fifth centuries A.D. as Christianity made its influence felt across the ancient world. For nearly two thousand years burial was established as the normal mode of dealing with human bodies once they had died. In this there was a complete symbolic consonance. What the Bible said in the Book of Genesis about Man made from the dust of the ground matched numerous Old Testament accounts of burial and gained added significance from the New Testament treatment of the death of Jesus. St. Paul's extensive reflections on the first and second Adam theme in both the Epistle to the Romans and First Corinthians related the death and resurrection of Christ to the death of Adam and the death of ordinary christians. The human body was as vital a sign of sin as of grace. Death overtook the body because of sin and it would be counteracted by a resurrection on the last day. As the death of the body was a sign of sin so its resurrection would be a sign of grace. The fact that Christ had been buried and was then resurrected provided a scheme which the faithful believer could expect to be repeated in his own case.

Since religious symbolism is an extremely complex process of human reflection it was possible for death and burial to carry numerous ideas along with it. On the one hand death resulted from sin and man returned to the dust whence he had come: this truly reflected the Genesis accounts. But on the other hand New Testament material focused on the dead body as the basis for the new resurrection body. On this count little thought was given to the fact of human dissolution. So the Genesis emphasis was on the end of all flesh while the New Testament emphasis fell upon the potential of what had been buried. Funerary ritual was easily able to carry both these symbolic meanings with burial a demonstrably clear symbol of the twofold Christian theology of death.

Given the intricate relationship between Jewish and Christian origins it is right that in a Christian theological reflection on death some thought be given to traditional Jewish interpretations. Although statements about an afterlife are not to be found in Jewish scriptures a strong interpretative tradition focused on resurrection emerged in rabbinic Judaism and were current at the time of Jesus. It has been argued recently that Jewish ideas of the afterlife emerged not through doctrinal debate as such but through discussion of death ritual and rules of mourning which Jewish communities developed over time,(Abramovitch 1985:132).

In contemporary Orthodox Jewish life in Jerusalem, for example, the body is seen as returning to the dust in accordance with Genesis while the soul is thought to return to God on the basis of Job 1:21 ,'The Lord has given and the Lord has taken away, blessed be the Name of the Lord.' Burial very rapidly follows death, preferably on the same day, and is carried out through a Burial Society of Orthodox believers who perform these rites for the dead. It is thought that only through contact with the soil can the pollution of the corpse be overcome. There is no coffin, only a shroud, a fact that some Israelis of American or Western European origin can find hard to accept. It also seems to be the case that the Orthodox rites clash with secular Israeli attitudes especially as far as ideas of rewards and punishments in the after-life are concerned, ideas which are expressed in the official funeral rites not least in collecting money for charity at the graveside. Some secular Israelis have developed their own 'funeral within the funeral' to add personal comments on the dead and to express individualized grief, (Abramovich 1986: 127 ff.) Cremation in this Orthodox context is unacceptable, unlike the situation in Britain where Liberal Jews do practise cremation.

SYMBOLS AND DEATH

From both a theological and anthropological perspective symbols may be said to participate in what they represent. Burial itself is a symbol and an extremely potent one both in the Jewish context just mentioned and in the more familiar case of Christianity. What happens in burial is not simply a manipulation of signs refering to emotions and religious attitudes. It also involves acts and thoughts which penetrate each other to touch the very heart of human nature which we culturally share. It is worth stressing the Jewish fact just mentioned that beliefs about the afterlife emerged through interpretation of funeral rites, 'ritualized theology in action' as Henry Abramovich, the Jewish American scholar and member of a Jerusalem Burial Society, described the process (1965:132). Anglicans should bear this in mind since rites often form the basis for popular religious understanding. Practice produces policy, rites yield popular theology. This is why symbols are important since they are vehicles for thought.

So, for example, burial participates in the dust theme but also has a future potential. The model of Christ's death underpins ordinary Christian burial and enhances its symbolic capacity. The burial of each ordinary individual is made potentially extraordinary by being associated with Christ's death and burial.

Traditionally speaking the power of Christian burial is reinforced as the idea of Christ's burial is set within the total history of mankind. For Christian Britain proper death rites have meant burial because the sacred texts of our culture history always stressed both the earth and burial as natural events. The idea of cremation was known, but as a practice of other cultures, most especially of India. Indeed the fact that the Indian practice was well known as a result of Britain's Imperial presence in the subcontinent is worth emphasizing because cremation could so easily be interpreted as a pagan activity, especially when associated with customs like that of the cremation of widows on their husbands funeral pyres (Geertz 1983:37 ff. for a cognate Balinese example).

As the Church of England rather rapidly came to accept cremation as a suitable funerary rite it acknowledged the difficulties which some people had over the strangeness of the idea. We have mentioned Forder's manual for Anglican priests with its general support of cremation.He also observed that some people dislike the idea of flames and fire, and are apt to misunderstand the 'refining fire' in terms of the 'everlasting fire'. Forder suggested that cremation ought perhaps to occur rather privately with only a male relative or two in attendance and that the ashes should then be brought into church for a committal service and for the interment of ashes. He pinpointed two problems with this scheme. The time taken for the cremation itself and the ceremonial problem of carrying ashes in an urn in any dignified way (1947:310).

What is obvious in Forder is the symbolic contradiction between cremation and burial. It seems to be a rite which itself is undergoing a change. From the single burial of the whole body we pass to the two-fold cremation of the body and burial of its ashes. A still more recent step seems to shift emphasis from the burial of ashes to the cremation event itself. In this scheme burial decreases as the cremation increases in significance. Even so the position of cremated remains is an important issue which cannot be ignored even though the cremation service comes to be the major focus. This is critical, for example, in cases where there is very little indeed left to cremate, as with newborn babies. It seems that parents are unhappy that nothing should be left to bury or scatter. This raises a problem of symbolism and attitudes. Cremation of everything, were it possible, would probably be quite undesirable, since ashes are one foundation for memory and for the identity of the dead in the recollection of the living.

With such symbolic concerns in mind we now leave these introductory points on history and theology and move to practical dimensions of cremation in faith and life: issues which are becoming increasingly significant given the British population profile in which the number dying will increase in the beginning of the next century and are likely to be cremated in increasing proportions.

1. Resurrection and Eternal Life

We begin empirically with views of rural populations in the five dioceses of Durham, Lincoln, Southwell, Gloucester, and Truro as fully presented in Volume IV of the Rural Church Project entitled *The Views of Rural Parishioners* (D. J. Davies *et. al.* 1990). Random samples of people on civic and church electoral rolls were interviewed during 1989.

To develop our analysis we add to the Rural Church Project further material drawn from The Cremation Research Project involving extensive interview data gathered from populations within the County of Nottingham. It provides a suburban and city balance to the rural findings. In the first instant we shall compare the findings on Reincarnation.

REINCARNATION

In the material gathered for the Rural Church Project the idea of reincarnation met with 12% agreement, 20% uncertainty, and 56% disagreement as far as the general public was concerned. The church electoral roll members showed only 4% agreement, with 18% uncertainty, and 69% disagreement. So the more active the church involvement the less likely people were to believe in what is an intrinsically non-Christian idea. Still, nearly a quarter of those on electoral rolls of churches were either unsure of this point or believed in it; this might mean that some discussion of the theme within a programme of church teaching might be worthwhile. Having said that, we do need to be cautious in interpreting such a high degree of support for reincarnation since in the The Cremation Research Project focused entirely in the County of Nottingham only 3% supported reincarnation. The reason for caution is twofold, one touching earlier research results, and another the rural context of the 12% RCP finding.

Geoffrey Gorer carried out two famous studies on aspects of religion in Britain involving surveys conducted in 1950 and 1963. In the 1950 survey less than 1% mentioned reincarnation while in 1963 just over 2% did so, (Gorer 1965:167). It is quite possible than by the late nineteen-eighties views on reincarnation had become increasingly popular so as to give the relatively high response rate of the Rural Church Project. But an additional factor may be involved in that with the Cremation Research Project there was a slight tendency for rural dwellers to support cremation more than their urban counterparts, (4.4% to 2.7%). Particular geographical areas of the country may also be responsible for a higher response rate than in Nottinghamshire.

CREMATION AND DISBELIEF IN AFTERLIFE

We do not possess this kind of survey evidence from earlier centuries on issues such as belief in life after death. Historians and some theologians assume that over recent centuries belief in an afterlife with its full scenario of heaven, hell, judgement and the like has declined quite dramatically. The hints present in what statistics we have do suggest a movement into disbelief and perhaps a reduction in uncertainty.

Philippe Aries, for example, in his study *Western Attitudes Towards Death From the Middle Ages to the Present,* is certain that a shift into disbelief has occurred, so much so that he regards cremation in Britain along with the practice of dispersing ashes as a 'desire to break with Christian tradition; it is a manifestation of enlightenment, of modernity' (1974:91).

While open to criticism this opinion is worth pondering because of the potential consequences for the clergy. It might even be argued that cremation services foster disbelief in the resurrection. At first glance such a suggestion would seem odd, for do not cremation services assume the resurrection of Jesus as their very foundation? Indeed they do in a formal sense. But the way people interpret ritual occasions, including the words of services, does not always correspond with the meaning intended by the officiant. I have explored this area of what I call dual purpose ritual elsewhere (Davies 1990:48). The essential point is that people take from ritual much of what they bring to it and much of what they intend through it. This sometimes conflicts with the outlook of the officiant as the representative of established religion. The rites of passage of marriage and infant baptism are two classic occasions for such dissonance between some clergy and people.

Cremation services could be fostering disbelief in the doctrine of the resurrection because of the implied assumption that resurrection has to do with graves and cremation has practically nothing to do with graves. I have no statistical evidence to justify this more speculative idea that has emerged around the research. Individuals are quick to construct their own meaning of rites, eliminating inappropriate ideas and incorporating viable ones. There are aspects of cremation services which do not seem to add up. There is a symbolic contradiction between the resurrection language taken from the old burial rite and the fact of cremation. This may well be why the treatment of ashes is paradoxical.

BODIES, IDENTITY AND RESURRECTION
In the Alternative Service Book of the Church of England there is both a funeral service and also a form to be used for the interment of ashes. In symbolic terms these two services present a potential confusion.

In the funeral rite the body is committed to be cremated in sure and certain hope of the resurrection, while in the subsequent rite the ashes are also committed to the ground in sure and certain hope of the resurrection. In other words both the fire and the earth are ritual moments of committal: the same thing happens twice. It is no wonder that people may be confused over what happens when. The ritual focus shifts and there is no sense of flow between what happens to the dead body and what happens to the ashes. Ritually speaking the ashes are treated in the same way as a body is treated and this I suggest is very likely to be a mistake. It is almost analogous to a category mistake in more logical forms of argument because in symbolic and emotional terms the ashes are not the body and the body is not ashes.

In the forms of analysis that anthropologists have used for death and funerary rites the dead body belongs to a different logical order of things than do its dry bones or ashes. One of the first and most influential of scholars involved in this field was Robert Hertz who did for funerary rites what Arnold Van Gennep did for the idea of rites of passage. Hertz (1907) explored the meaning of funerary rites in societies which had what he called a double burial, where the body was initially treated in one way and where its subsequent remains were treated in another. His basic argument was that the human body carries an identity with it and this has to shift from that of the living person to that of, for example, an ancestor. An initial burial witnesses the decline of the old identity, while a second burial or relocation of the bones or ashes initiates the new identity as ancestor. Through such rites a person is moved from the realm of the living to the realm of the departed. Mourning rites mirror this shift in the identity of the dead.

Hertz felt that such double burials differed significantly from the western Christian cultural form where there was but one burial associated with the belief that immediately at death the soul appears before God. Hertz pointed out that non-western cremation is seldom a single act but is usually the first part of a double mortuary rite in which the second phase involves a locating of the remains in an ancestral context. In his passing comment I think that Hertz provides us with a significant key to the problematic nature of cremation within western and traditionally Christian cultures.

The symbolic dissonance between burial and cremation lies precisely in the fact that attitudes towards the dead body and attitudes towards ashes are different. The difference is related to the identity of the deceased person and the relationship of the living towards that dead person. The dead body carries the identity of the deceased in an immediate way. It is specifically his or her body, capable of evoking a personal response from the survivors. The ashes present a less personal, more distanced, identity of the deceased. Ashes do not evoke emotion in the same way as the dead body, or even as a grave does, they represent what might be called a post-person state of the deceased.

Indeed it seems as though there is a difference perceived between burial and cremation on this very point. Of the individuals interviewed about the emotional dimension of funerals 43% thought there was no basic difference between burial and cremation. Of the rest the great majority thought that burial was a more emotional experience than was cremation. This raises the question of the therapeutic nature of emotion at funerals, an issue which is problematic because surrounded by particular social values. There are those who say that a funeral rite should encourage the bereaved to cry and display emotion, in fact this is almost stated as a psychologically important fact in some English middle class groups. But others regard a display of emotion as wrong.

EMOTIONAL DISPLAY

The key phrase in this discussion is 'display', for displays are social acts and need practice and experience, while in modern British society many have but little experience of how to display emotion. Indeed some young people said that they simply did not know how to behave at a crematorium let alone know how to display an appropriate emotion. The public world of social behaviour and the private world of grief are not, at present, particularly well correlated in England. Although we have very little evidence for saying it, it might be suggested, that there are important social class and regional differences on these very points. The view that grief should be 'let out' through the funeral rite may indicate more about certain popular concepts of psychology in particular segments of the population than of a universal truth. For some a contained presence may well be far more sustaining.

The fact that cremation can result in no grave is welcomed by a small group of people who want to have a death over and done with and who do not want a place to visit for memorial purposes. The popular idea that it is important to have a place in relation to which mourning may occur is not uniformly accepted. Generalizations are not particularly useful in this area of emotional and social life. Attitudes to ashes and body are complex. But there is one dimension which must finally be mentioned and which adds a further dimension to the analysis of the identity of human remains.

In ritual and symbolic terms the body is cremated in a public and more open ceremony while the ashes, if treated at all, are handled in a more private and personal ceremony. In other words the more personal symbol, the body, is treated less personally while the less personal symbol, the ashes, is treated more personally.

ALTERNATIVE SERVICE BOOK AND THE COMMITTALS

As already indicated, the funeral services in the Alternative Service Book are relatively unclear on these issues, which is understandable since systematic theology itself has said little about the problem. This is why I suggest that ministers may actually encourage disbelief in the doctrine of the resurrection because the services they use also encourage an uncertainty of intention. The actual words used give ample scope for interpreting human life in terms of a body-soul dichotomy, and where such a dichotomy exists it is likely that the actual idea of resurrection gives way to that of perpetual souls continuing into a heavenly realm. The deceased is committed into God's 'merciful keeping' while the body or ashes are committed to the ground or to be cremated. The easy implication is that the earthy bits are earthed while the life as such passes on into God's keeping.

If the formal doctrinal intent is to argue for a soul then the words of the service have a point to them, but if no soul-doctrine is intended then the words need clarification to make the point that nobody possesses an intrinsic life-force but rather must await God's creative power. Even so the double use of the idea of committal both to cremation and then of the ashes to the ground requires some attention.

The clergy of Southwell Diocese were asked if they associated the committal with the cremation service itself or with the interment of ashes? The great majority (80%) clearly saw the committal as at the cremation itself. Approximately 6% focused on the burial of ashes, while the remainder thought it depended on other factors such as the last occasion when the priest was involved with the remains. One individual said he had no clear and thought out view of the issue, a point which may also be reflected in the fact that on this one question the respondents often ticked one answer only to cross it out and suggest another.

ASHES

There is no prescribed treatment for all ashes, much is left to the surviving relatives. Those interviewed in Nottinghamshire showed approximately 11%

who had thought about the placing of ashes prior to death. It would seem that the majority have to decide what to do with the ashes after the actual cremation. When asked if they had done the correct thing with the ashes about half thought they had, 11% thought they had not, while about a third were unsure. This suggests that more opportunity to discuss these issues should be provided and certainly suggests that there is a degree of hit-and-miss involved in the present situation. When asked what they wished to happen to their own ashes the largest response, 42% in all, was one of uncertainty. This may be one reason why an earlier discussion might be useful, to help clarify the question, but for some it is a difficult issue to approach. Still, 34% did know and wished their remains to be scattered or buried at a particular place, while 19% simply assumed they would be scattered somewhere. Scattering at sea was the choice of 3%.

Little formal attention has been paid to what is sometimes done with ashes despite many stories, anecdotes and a genre of jokes about their location. In surveys of British Crematoria and clergy we found numerous accounts of special requests for ashes. These included a request that half of one person's ashes should be scattered on the ground while the other half be taken home; that ashes be scattered from an aircraft, from an oil-tanker at sea, be emptied into a mine-shaft, be scattered on a football-pitch, on bowling greens, down the middle of a particular high street of a town, and on a traffic island in the middle of the road-way. One individual, an ardent gambler, had betting slips and a copy of the *Sporting Life* placed in his coffin and after cremation his ashes were scattered over a racecourse (*Pharos* Vol 55, NO 3, P.124).

Very many of these special requests or appropriate placing of ash-remains indicate some habit or special interest of the deceased: they are marks of life identity. They refer to life rather than to the after-life and in this run counter to any orthodox Christian idea of God's act in relation to that person's future state.In many respects the final resting place is a fulfilment of wishes or desires in life, it is a kind of extension of the 'retirement home in the country'. The identity expressed by such special placing is not eschatological but a fulfilment of 'this-worldly' ideas.

It is such a 'this-worldly' orientation that may lie behind the desire to have a fixed location for the burial of remains giving a sense of the location of the deceased and providing a context for a continuing relationship with the deceased. It seems to be more the case with body burial but also to some extent with the burial of ashes that survivors visit the grave, ostensibly to tidy it, but perhaps even more importantly to pray and to talk to the dead person. The notion of keeping the grave tidy or of bringing flowers is a socially acceptable reason for regular visits whereas it would be very socially and emotionally difficult to tell people one was visiting the grave to communicate with the deceased. Yet this seems to be the case for a considerable minority. This is an important pastoral fact in connection with bureaucratic ideals of lawn-like cemeteries.

Much more work needs to be done on these questions since they touch on the growth in individualism in contemporary culture and the move away from traditional schemes of belief in which many, if not all, shared.

2. Pastoral Practice and Cultural Life

The key question for this chapter is whether clergy are likely to become increasingly redundant as officiants at Cremation services?

It is often argued that British society is becoming increasingly secularized with religious ideas counting for less in both public and private life. Since crematoria are institutions under local authority or private company ownership rather than being church institutions it would be quite reasonable to expect secular ideas to become apparent within this particular domain.

To explore this possibility we asked people in the surveys several particular questions. The first was the obvious one of whether funerals should generally be conducted by clergy. Of the five diocese rural survey we found that 85% of the general public thought clergy should conduct funerals, 11% thought not, 4% refused or did not know. As might be expected a higher percentage of those on church electoral rolls supported clergy as officiants, in fact 91% did so. Some 4% disagreed and 5% refused or did not know. Still there is the suggestion here that for some 15% of the general public the issue is an open one and other people could well be acceptable as officiants. There were no gender differences on this question. In terms of age group we found that those aged 35-44 gave the lowest support for clerical officiants at 75%. These results were, of course, obtained from rural areas of Britain where more traditional and established views might be anticipated.

Fortunately we can balance this evidence against urban and rural material from the Cremation Research Project in Nottinghamshire. The question put to these individuals was more open than that of the Rural Church survey and simply asked who should conduct funeral services. In response 73% preferred the clergy, 2% were happy with crematorium staff,while 7% opted for friends. This Nottingham result suggests that in general about three quarters of the general public prefer clergy as officiants. When looked at in geographical terms the highest support for the clergy was in the most rural village surveyed (87%), a figure practically identical to that of the Rural Church Survey, while the lowest (61%) was in one of two large suburban areas surveyed. In this the rural factor does seem significant. But the question of social class is probably also significant in that the more working class of the two suburbs studied had a 3.5% support for crematorium officials as officiants, a figure matching that of the rural village which also had a strong working class element. Another village studied, which has a much higher preponderance of professional and commuting personnel did not even make a 1% support for this idea. Again it is important to stress that these low figures represent *unsolicited* mention of crematorium personnel.

When people were specifically asked if undertakers or crematorium officials should be allowed to conduct cremation services, as they were asked on the national five diocese Rural Church survey, a different profile of response emerged as one would anticipate. What is perhaps surprising is that there was practically no difference between civic (25% yes—67% no) and church electoral roll members (24% yes—65% no) on this question.

These results tell a similar story to the earlier findings in suggesting that perhaps a quarter of the public would not be unhappy if undertakers or crematorium staff conducted funeral rites. But the obverse is that a large majority would not like the practice, the young and the middle-aged being particularly opposed.

It was also the case that the two oldest groups had the highest level of uncertainty on the issue with 11% of the over-55-year-olds, and 14% of the over-65-year-olds not being sure about the question. Popular opinion might have expected the elderly to be more adamant in a traditional direction about these matters, but this was not the case. On numerous issues we found that older people were more open to possibilities and practices concerning death than were younger people. This is probably due to their greater variety of experience since age and familiarity with funerals are positively related.

With this in mind it is particularly interesting to ask what clergy think about officiants at cremations. The question was put to the clergy in the Diocese of Southwell and 5% thought non-clerical officiants a good idea, while a further 27% were unsure. Some clergy are obviously somewhat ambivalent over their performance of certain cremations. But many more expressed a degree of certainty that people definitely wanted clergy to perform their rites. If the above evidence for the laity is at all representative of popular thought then a significant minority of clergy seem to underestimate the public's relative though limited open-mindedness.

CLERICAL REDUNDANCY?
We are now able to answer our opening question whether clerical redundancy might result from increased secularization of funerary rites? Since clergy currently conduct the very great majority of funerary rites at crematoria and since the samples surveyed here seem to stick at about 70% support for the clergy it would seem that there is the possibility of about 25% of the population being content with people other than clergy conducting funeral rites. This would involve a major change of custom, but when it is remembered that the growth of cremation has advanced so rapidly within forty years no social change can be denied. Such a change may occur again on the pastoral front. Funeral Directors and others in the area of servicing death are well aware of the pastoral needs surrounding bereavement. They have a profit motive as is inevitable in business people,but many of them are also very aware of their professional ethos and of the care that people need in connection with bereavement and grief.

FUNERAL DIRECTORS, CLERGY, AND LAY PASTORAL INVOLVEMENT?
It would be relatively easy for a Funeral Agency to cover all aspects of bereavement, not simply by employing clergy as a specialist agent but by arranging funerals in which a non-clerical individual conducted the service in which family and friends were encouraged to participate. A follow up service of counselling could also be provided along with advice on financial and legal matters, issues which the clergy will often have neither the expertise nor time to cover. Given the fact that such Funeral Agencies would have this as their prime business they would become much more effective and thorough in it than many clergy who

have numerous other concerns, and for whom the cremation or burial of people entirely outside their actual congregations is a marginal activity.

If churches genuinely view funeral activities as part of their proper business and as within the total scope of pastoral care and pastoral evangelism, then the question of adequate provision over bereavement needs to be high on the church agenda. It may be that the earlier period of crematorium rotas of clerical duty has properly soured some attitudes towards planning in this particular area. Still it should, perhaps, be a major issue especially for large city and town areas where teams of clergy and suitably trained laity could operate.

This point about the laity is important. The fact that a large minority of the general public seems open to the idea that people other than clergy might conduct funerals could spur church organization into using the pastoral gifts of the laity, and perhaps not only of Readers, in the case of the Church of England, in so doing.

FUNERALS AND FAITH

In the Cremation Research Project a small group of people were interviewed at some length on many aspects of cremation. One fact emerging from this was that 13% said their religious faith had been strengthened through the events surrounding death and cremation, while nearly 2% said that their faith had actually been initiated at that time. A further 5%, on the contrary, said their faith had been weakened. This suggests that practically a fifth of those interviewed were undergoing some significant sort of religious change of outlook and might have benefited from more extensive pastoral care. Many, of course, said how they did gain from the services of the clergy. In the Rural Church survey 68% of civic and 83% of church electoral roll members said they would request clergy assistance over periods of bereavement. There is no guarantee that such a response would be reproduced in more urban contexts, indeed in the Nottinghamshire study we asked people if they would value a visit from a priest in the period following a cremation service, we found that the traditional rural village setting expressed the highest acceptance of this service (54%), while a large suburban area had only just over a third of its respondents (35%) keen on such a visit. The question of social class is probably important here too, for we found that a higher proportion (45%) of a more middle class suburb felt the need of clergy during bereavement.

What is perhaps surprising about these results is that the acceptance of this sort of contact with the clergy is not as high as might have been expected, given that clergy service practically all funerals. In terms of those who did not want to be visited the results showed approximately a third of a more working class suburb, but also a quarter of a more traditional rural village. Around 20% of individuals in most contexts were unsure about receiving a post-cremation visit.

The total sample, rural and urban, in Nottinghamshire showed a 46% welcome of the priest, a 32% wish not to be visited, with 22% not knowing which they preferred. And this for a sample in which 36% reckoned to practise their religion regularly, 26% occasionally, with 38% not practising any sort of public religion. This evidence presses further our earlier point about the scope for secular funeral services when we said that perhaps a quarter of the population might be open to the idea. The figure may even be higher, perhaps even a third of the population ?

SERVICES PROVIDED: TRADITION, SUPPLY AND DEMAND

Christian Churches have, historically, been involved in funerary ritual to very different degrees (J. G. Davies 1986:117 ff.), Sometimes they have sought to oppose local practice when it was perceived as pagan; at other times they have developed rites which complement local tradition (M. Bloch 1971).

Contemporary British culture has been deeply influenced by Christianity as far as its funerary rites are concerned. But times are changing and the future is open to major shifts in the form of funeral service. Much depends upon what is offered to people. Very many people think only in terms of a service by a clergyman, and funeral directors manage things in such a way that it is largely a foregone conclusion that clergy will conduct the service. But the issue of secular funerals is a lively one, and more than that, there is the question of funerals which are not avowedly secular but which are, for want of a better word, family and friend focused (Walter 1989).

PASTORAL EVANGELISM

If funeral directors presented their clients with the option of having a traditional funeral conducted by a priest or one managed by a funeral professional which incorporated some elements from family and friends this latter type of service might well attract a very significant minority of people. The issue of supply and demand is not irrelevant here. The active interest of the funeral professionals could easily produce a situation in which the clergy could be increasingly marginalized.

There are two possible responses to this. On the one hand some clergy would see the transformation as good in that it would allow actively committed Christians to have church focused funerals while others would not receive such treatment. This would mark out Christian from nominal Christian and allow the faith to be more distinctive. But, on the other hand, others would see this as a loss as far as the pastoral opportunity for care and evangelism was concerned.

In fact the theme of pastoral evangelism is very important for the Church of England in particular. The 'charitable assumption' of the Church of England which takes both baptized members and other parishioners as Christian for practical purposes is a powerful basis from which to engage in caring for people and educating them in basic Christianity. Pastoral evangelism is closely related to liturgy of many kinds. The education in faith that comes from involvement in the ritual life of a church must never be ignored. It may be that clergy learn much theology in a formal way, but many other people of varying degree of faith learn their religion through practical involvement; this is why it is important to have forms of religious service which encode Christian truth in ways which may be acquired by participants. Much religious knowledge is symbolic knowledge and is acquired almost implicitly over time rather than being explicitly taught (Sperber 1975). Hence the provision of a form of cremation service in the conclusion to this book.

3. The Body, Cremation, and the Church

The doctrines of creation and salvation ensure that the human body has a special place in Christian thought. The Incarnation and the Resurrection define the domain of human existence through the experience of Jesus and through the life experience of Christians. The bodies of the dead have, in turn, been treated with respect because of their identification with the body of Jesus and the hope of resurrection.

For those without such religious belief bodies still remain highly significant as the remains of loved ones. For both believer and unbeliever the dead are increasingly 'privatized'. Dead bodies are not left in sight of simply anyone. In the Nottinghamshire survey of older adults 42% had never seen a dead body. Cremation comes as a most appropriate process for such people, totally removing the body from the human and social world and leaving in its stead dry ashes which can be easily controlled and managed. The idea that the remains of a relative could be placed in a dozen matchboxes and divided amongst a family makes sense only for ashes and involves a logic that is quite impossible when considering a dead body (Barley 1989:113).

What to do with dead bodies is now an issue for everyone. There is choice. And there are levels of uncertainty over this choice. Pastorally speaking this is an important area especially in seeking to understand what people mean when they talk about cremation in relation to their deceased.

'Natural and clinical' are two ideas often expressed in discussions on cremation. One way of exploring their significance is by relating them to religion itself through the question 'Whether crematoria are religious places or not?'. In doing this we list some comments on funerals which will echo the experience of many readers and hint at what concerns many people over funerals, death, and the identity of their dead.

'Cremation is final,conclusive,cleaner. Burial is less final, less conclusive, less violent, gentler, more natural. I was at a cremation that had farcical processional music; almost comic descent of the coffin like a tasteless sketch on a comedy show.' (Female aged 21).

'It's nice for some to have their ashes scattered at a spot they were connected with, and for a close friend to do the scattering. The scattering must seem a good transition for the bereaved.' (Male aged 23).

'Cremation was impersonal, quick, and less emotional than burial. Cremation may be preferred by those without beliefs, for whom death is meaningless'. (Male aged 22).

'Bereavement was eased by a burial in a small graveyard behind the parish church. Buried in his mother's grave there was both parting (from the living) and re-uniting (with his mother) which eased the tragedy'. (Female aged 47).

'I would rather be buried. The thought of cremation for me is linked with evil and hell'. (Female aged 18).

'There is a definite need for a more secular funeral in our society which on the whole has disowned Christianity'.'The drive from the church to the crematorium was dire'.(Male aged 21).

Responses to this question are particularly interesting as far as the age of respondents is concerned. In the general survey in Nottinghamshire 52% thought crematoria were sacred, 37% did not think they were sacred, and 11% were unsure. This represents a group with only 1% under twenty years of age and with a relatively equal distribution over other age groups. But, in several different groups of students aged mostly twenty or under the attitude is different with, in one typical survey of a small group of forty three students drawn from a variety of academic subjects 30% thinking that crematoria were sacred, 47% thinking they were not, and 23% not knowing.

It is, of course, incredibly difficult to define the word 'religious' in any decisive way and it might be argued that young people belong to a secular society in which most things would not be regarded as sacred. But, if belief in life after death is any index of religiosity, we can say for this particular group of young people that 60% did believe in it, 21% did not, and 19% were unsure. Among those who did believe in life after death more said that crematoria were not religious places than accepted them as religious. It may be that personal religious belief was not the sole or perhaps even the most significant element in the evaluation made of crematoria. Two students who did not believe in an afterlife and who espoused a very clear scientific approach to human life still argued for crematoria being religious because they were places associated with the last rites of a human life and with the grief of mourners.

This mention of grief gets us closer to the meaning of 'religious' values in connection with crematoria. The 'religious' factor is deeply associated with human emotion and the worth of life. It is because the crematorium is associated with moments of deep personal emotion, even though that emotion may not be given a public display, that it attracts the idea of being a religious place. In many respects the classic idea of a sacred place has to do more with the experience of people than the intrinsic nature of the place itself. This, I think, is a better explanation of the difference between the responses of young and old towards crematoria. The young speak of crematoria in an abstract way since about a half had never been to one, and these individuals tended to be more certain in their judgement that crematoria are not religious places. Those who had been to a cremation service were almost equally divided on the subject including those whose minds were now more uncertain about the answer. Although we are dealing with relatively small numbers of students the pattern is of a piece with the much larger general Nottinghamshire survey in the sense that greater exposure to crematoria seems to induce a sense of significance attached to them. Indeed it is this very issue of personal emotional significance which may well be the basis for describing crematoria as religious places. This is an important point since in strictly theological terms we tend to start with God when defining ideas of religion, but when we move in the realm of people's experience it is always wise to consider other possible dynamics and dimensions.

Now that cremation has become the normal funeral mode of Britain and as families come to be associated with crematoria, especially particular local crematoria, we can expect this sense of religiosity to increase. To use the vague yet powerful word 'depth' we may suggest that as the depth of human experience in association with crematoria grows so will the sense of the sacredness of crematoria.

We are now in a position to see just how the 'religiousness' of crematoria is related to their 'clinical' nature. The starting point lies within human relationships and the 'relationship of bereavement', if we may so call one response to death. The emotion engendered by death is radically personal. It belongs to a sense of fellow feeling with other human beings, it involves love, fear, tears, and all that belongs to sympathy and empathy. In our culture it is historically the case that death is associated with nature. Death is the process by which a living individual becomes a dead body and that body returns to the earth until it finally merges with it in a process of time that is deemed natural. The 'speed' of the total death process is relatively slow. What is more the human input into the death process is relatively low. A coffin is made and a hole dug and the person's body is lowered into the earth. What happened to the body was, culturally, unimaginable. Whatever happened took place invisibly leaving the imagination to work as it might.

Modern cremation changed all this at a blow. In the most fundamental of symbolic senses cremation altered the 'speed' of the total death process. In one hour and a half the body becomes dust. This is a strictly imaginable period. Not only so but the human input into the process is extremely high. The crematorium is a technological processing plant, a kind of factory, yet it is never spoken of as such except insofar as people speak of the production line aspect of funerals lining up to use the premises. In this sense it is the diametrical opposite of the grave which is a hole into nature. In the old fashioned language of earth symbolism burial can be read as a return to mother nature. The crematorium, by contrast, is more like an entry into industrial technology. This, I suspect, is why the element of fire has had its naturalness robbed from it when it comes to cremation.

FIRE AS FURNACE
For the British fire is not a 'natural' element. Though we traditionally speak of earth, air, fire, and water, as natural elements we no longer perceive them all as such. Fire becomes unnatural when it is contained and, as it were, tamed. In cremation the process relates more to a furnace than to fire, and a furnace is very much an expression of technological control. It is the overall idea of human control of the dead body through fire which sets the key for the negative view of crematoria held by many younger people. In anthropological terms culture or human work takes over from nature in the process of death. And this is felt to be wrong by many younger people for whom death is a distant thing and yet which they think of in terms of natural processes rather than cultural processes.

There may also be an additional factor concerning the concrete fact that human beings actually set about the burning of other human beings. There may be many psychological issues here including the idea of cremation as violence done to the dead. One more certain aspect of the clinical and mechanical description of crematoria is the sense of hidden activity. In a crematorium all is not open to the public eye within the service itself.There actually is something going on behind the scenes, unlike the case of a graveyard where all believe they see all that there is to see. The existence of stories and jokes about crematoria indicates something of this awareness. Many people seem to believe that in crematoria many bodies are burned at once, that bodies are taken out of coffins which are reused, that the correct ashes are not retrieved, and so on. Crematorium authorities are very eager that the error of these statements be made fully known by increased public education through open days and clearer information.

Behind problems of cremation there lies a cultural history of fire in Britain which becomes all the clearer when compared with the place of fire in, for example, Indian cultural thought. In the Hindu scheme of reincarnation or transmigration of the soul fire fits perfectly into the process of personal change.Theological, mythical, and psychological facts fit each other in complementary assonance. The person is, technically, not dead until the skull is cracked during the cremation itself thus allowing the soul entry into its next phase of life. Fire is a fine medium for the message of the continuing soul. And here lies a paradox for western cremation.

Fire as a free agent is indeed an appropriate medium for the mobile soul, but fire as a contained entity, fire as a furnace, is not so appropriate. In British culture, or perhaps it might be better to say in modern British folk-lore, the fire is more likely to be interpreted in relation to smoke and smell and in this sense to the bodily and material aspect of life rather than to the spiritual dimension. It is within the imagination that fire can be thought of as a vehicle for freeing the soul or aiding its departure, but within Christian theology fire has tended to have negative symbolic value. It is associated with the fire of hell, or with the burning of heretics. The notion of a purifying fire is itself not entirely positive. Sometimes there is also a hint of the role of cremation in the burning of bodies during the Nazi Holocaust. What is the more astonishing then is the fact that despite these symbolic, aesthetic, and theological issues cremation has become established as the primary British form of funeral.

As this is true historically so it is true that familiarity throughout life brings many people to a changed outlook on cremation, even though it takes time. Research on another student group of some 73 students found an interestingly significant difference between them. Those who had never attended a funeral stated that their personal choice was for cremation, but those who had been to both one cremation and one burial chose burial. Only a long term study of the same group could prove that change takes place over time, but as our knowledge now stands it looks as though attitudes to cremation change as people grow older and gain more first-hand experience of cremation services. This is the case in the Rural Church material where in the laity survey the percentage of those favouring cremation was related to age in the following way: 34% for 18-34 years, 45% for 35-44 years, 42% for 45-54 years, 49% for 55-64 years, and also 49% for those over 65% . The theoretical issues of this chapter have paved the way for a more empirical study of the views of clergy and people to which we now turn.

4. Clerical and Lay Views

What do clergy and laity think about cremation ? How do their views differ ? How does the eucharist relate to the Communion of Saints and to knowledge of the dead? What are the consequences for pastoral theology and care? These central questions of this chapter are explored by comparing rural material drawn from the Rural Church Project with more urban-focused data from Nottinghamshire covered in The Cremation Research Project.

SOME BASIC FACTS

Comparing the views of rural clergy with those of a cross-section of the rural community and of church members covered in the Rural Church Report in the four dioceses of Lincoln, Southwell, Gloucester, and Truro, we found the following choices on burial and cremation.

Table 2.1 Funeral Choice of Rural Public and Clergy		
Choice	Public	Clergy
Cremation	46	32
Burial	31	27
Don't Mind	23	41
Total %	100	100

The difference between rural Anglican churchgoers and the general public at large is very small on these matters so there is no need to separate them from each other in comparison with the clergy. The one exception to this generalization occurs amongst non-Anglican church attenders, largely composed of Methodists and Roman Catholics. Of these 50% preferred burial and only 18% opted for cremation, while 32% didn't mind or know which they wanted. While the Methodist and Roman Catholic reasons for this preferred pattern probably vary, both reflect a more traditional funerary preference.

In Table 2.1 there is an interesting difference between rural clergy and people, with the clergy having a lower preference for cremation than the public at large but also having a much higher sense of not caring about the question. The fact that practically twice as many clergy were unconcerned about this question than were the laity at large is noteworthy. During interview the clergy often showed a basic disregard for this aspect of their own life and in one way it mirrored their attitude to retirement and housing plans for that later period in their life. Exactly 27% of the rural clergy owned houses in readiness for retirement and exactly 27% wished to be buried: further analysis will show whether the individuals making these plans were identical!

It might well be that familiarity with both cremation and burial induces a lack of interest in the clergy's personal choice of funeral. But another interpretation is also possible. In a separate study of clergy in the Diocese of Southwell there was a much lower incidence of indecision over this question. In the Southwell study the clergy answering the questionnaire included urban and inner-city pastors as well as some rural clergy. Because of this the following table probably gives a better view of clergy at large than does the specifically rural material.

Table 2.2 Funeral Choice of Clergy and People of Southwell		
	Clergy	People
Cremation	47	55
Burial	27	17
Don't Know	26	28
Total %	100	100

One interesting comparison between the Southwell clergy and the rural clergy of Table 2.1 is that 27% of each wish to be buried. More Southwell clergy (47%) want to be cremated than do the rural clergy of the Rural Church survey (32%). The mixed Nottinghamshire population have a relatively low (17%) desire for burial compared with the rural laity (31%).

Returning to the issue of indecision over funeral mode the striking feature is that the Southwell clergy have a relatively low level of uncertainty (26%), which is practically identical to that of their people, while the clergy in the Rural Church survey have a very high level of uncertainty (41%) which is nearly twice that of their people. This may suggest that the Southwell clergy, many of whom serve in urban areas, share popular attitudes to a greater extent than do their rural counterparts. Given the shared level of commitment to burial the high level of indecision among rural clergy suggests that they may be in the process of following their more urban colleagues in opting for cremation.

All this indicates a degree of difference between clergy and people over cremation and burial and might be useful information as clergy reflect on their pastoral involvement in funerals. To the same end it is also important to have some idea of the attitudes, especially the fears, that a significant minority of people express in relation to cremation and burial, to which we now turn.

SOME FEARS OF DEATH AND FUNERALS
In the Nottinghamshire survey the great majority of people (79%) said they had no particular fears and worries about cremation and burial. By and large more people were concerned about how they might die than about any subsequent consequences for themselves. In the light of the fact that cremation is now the normal funerary mode it is important to note that 8% said they feared being burnt alive. Only 3% said they disliked the idea of rotting in the ground or being eaten by worms. The fear of being burnt alive seems to have replaced the fear of being buried alive which was often said to be a worry earlier days. Concern over having an unattended grave in the future gained less than 1% response, while fear of the wrong ashes being allocated to relatives stood at 1.5%. All in all fears associated with cremation have replaced fears of burial as might be expected in the altered primacy of cremation over burial in Britain.

CREMATION, SOCIAL CLASS AND IDENTITY
In terms of popular opinion both burial and cremation are thought by over half the Nottingham population (56%) to be equally employed as funeral rites. But

just under a half of the population thinks that there is a class preference. Some 30% think that upper classes bury more often than they cremate, while 11% think that the upper classes cremate more often than they bury.

When asked the direct question of which they thought should be the mode of funeral for the British Monarch the results reinforce the idea that upper classes bury more than they cremate and also shows a clear inversion of what people wish for themselves as the following Table shows.

Table 2.3 Own and Royal Funeral		
Preference	Self	Queen
Burial	31	48
Cremation	44	19
Undecided	25	33
Total	100%	100%

This difference between personal wishes and thoughts for the Monarch's funeral are quite stark and statistically very significant. They indicate how rapidly social practice has changed on this one item of national life and how it is perceived to contradict to some extent the established and historical pattern of funerary activity, (Gittings 1984:216). But it is important to draw attention to the undecided category of respondents because it is they who indicate something of the social change affecting funerary customs. That a third of those questioned should be undecided on what could be regarded as a fixed social custom is very significant. When people were asked the reason for their view on royal funerals a third (31%) gave no reason, 28% thought it was a question of tradition, 15% thought it depended upon the monarch and her family's wishes, while 14% thought that everyone should be cremated.

THE FUNERAL OF A STILL-BORN BABY
Another question asked of the Nottinghamshire general public was whether they thought it better to bury or to cremate a baby which was born dead? Some 48% opted for cremation, 26% for burial, and 26% did not know. By and large these responses matched people's wishes for their own funeral except that there is a slightly greater emphasis on cremation and less on burial.It is interesting to compare the reasons given for choices over the monarch and the still-born baby as outlined in the following table which has been organized in such a way as to parallel items expressing very similar ideas in different ways.

Table 2.4 Monarch and Still-Birth Funerals			
Reason	Monarch	Still-Birth	
Cremation for all	14	15	
Save Land	2	6	
Family Choice	15	8	
(Tradition)	28	(Sensitivity)	7
Tomb Memorial	10	(Lest Forget)	20
Don't Know	31	44	
Total Percent	100%	100%	

The acknowledged place of tradition in Royal Burials is matched by the idea of sensitivity over the still-birth, the idea being taken up in the strong belief (20%) that it would be easy to forget a still-birth if the child is cremated. The Mausoleum or tomb of the monarch represents a similar idea of a continuing memory. The role of saving land through cremation occupies a relatively low profile in this case. In many contexts the issue of saving land tended not to arise until the issue was specifically addressed and then, as we have shown, some 63% accept the assumption that cremation involves a saving of land. For most people personal matters of memory lie closer to heart than does land use.

MEMORY, THE DEAD, AND EUCHARISTIC LITURGY

There are few areas about which we know less than that of religious experience in relation to liturgy. But information does exist, and it is, perhaps, surprising.

We begin, once more, in dependence upon material drawn from The Rural Church Project in which communicant churchgoers were asked what the Holy Communion service meant for them. They were presented with different statements including one asking whether they gained a sense of the presence of dead loved ones during the eucharist:

Table 2.5 Sense of Dead Loved Ones and Age					
Age	18-34	35-44	45-54	55-64	65+
%	50	39	31	27	47

Both the younger and older sets of adults shared a very similar response of about half those questioned. In the middle-aged and older middle-aged it dropped to just between a third and a quarter. It would be valuable to have further research information on this important topic to see if such a result would be gained repeatedly. From the available information it might be argued that a sense of presence of dead loved ones makes an impact on individuals earlier in their life but then declines in significance as age and other experiences and events impose themselves, but then in older age as death comes to spouses the experience once more becomes significant.

One other study of religious experience, conducted in Nottinghamshire on a largely urban sample, (Hay and Morisy 1985) found 22% reporting the presence or help of the deceased. The authors stress the smallness of their sample which was approximately a fifth of the Rural Church Project, and a quarter of the Cremation Research Project sample size. So with added caution we mention one point they made, that more people (61%) thought this sense of presence had only slightly influenced their own life or had not influenced it at all, compared with the minority (39%) who thought the experience had influenced their own lives. Unlike Hay and Morisy the Rural Church study found practically no difference between men and women on this count, it also found that the sense of the dead is not particularly closely linked to the idea of ghosts,(Cf. Finucane 1982). Some 19% on church electoral rolls, and 29% on civic rolls reckoned to believe in ghosts. There was practically no difference between men and women on this issue, but it was clearly the case that older individuals were much less likely to believe in ghosts than were young people.

Such evidence gives cause for reflection on the fact that Eucharistic liturgy gives clear place to the general belief in the Communion of Saints, and specific mention of those who are dying or who have just died. It embraces the fact that spirituality is extremely complex and for individuals entails their whole life experience. Personal spirituality interacts with the public symbolic life of Christian liturgy in a very creative way. The liturgy of the church embedding the Christian message as it does inevitably engages with death. The Christian religion, more than any other, has death centrally located in its worship. The eucharist celebrates the death of Jesus, while the central period of the Passion of Christ attendant upon Easter does the same. Christians are bidden to enter into Christ's death through these events as they are also bidden to do in baptism.

Of course it is also the case that resurrection goes hand in hand with each focus on death, but during life we have more experience of actual death than of actual resurrection which makes it understandable that the death elements might naturally come to the fore. The fact that a considerable number of people say they attend church the week following a funeral might well reinforce the association between memory of the dead and church services. This is perfectly in accord with theories of symbolic learning which talk of the cumulative way in which experiences integrate with each other over time (Sperber 1975).

DREAMS AND EXPERIENCE OF THE DEAD
Since human experience exists as a single reality for each person it is pastorally important to relate experience gained in liturgy to experience gained elsewhere, not least as far as memory of the dead is concerned. For the information we have to turn to the Cremation Research Project and to the 62 individuals interviewed in depth about their experience.

First we asked about dreams and found that 37% had dreamed about the deceased individual some time after the funeral. Of those who decided to comment on the nature of these dreams the majority found them neutral as far as mood was concerned. But nearly a quarter found them pleasing and only 3% said the dream was bad. When it came to the question of the appearance of the deceased in dreams, most had nothing to say or failed to respond; still 23% said the deceased appeared alive and well.

Another sort of experience comes in the waking state rather than when asleep and was reported by 45% of those interviewed which means that for our relatively small group of 62 interviewees more actually reported these waking experiences than sleeping experiences. Some 27% reported a sense of presence, 11% said they actually saw the deceased, while about 6% heard or spoke to the deceased. When it came to exploring reasons for the encounter only about 11% felt they could make any real comment, but all of these were positive and reinforced a sense of well being either of the deceased or else of the living. Despite its tentative and sketchy nature this material indicates areas of pastoral concern and care which could be of great use over bereavement. It also shows how private experience may well integrate with both the eucharistic and funerary liturgy of the church.

5. Theology of Cremation

It was probably inevitable that cremation services should develop from the traditional burial service through simple modifications. The unfortunate inference that can too easily be drawn from this is that there is no fundamental distinction to be made between burial and cremation. But cremation raises fundamental theological and symbolic questions more starkly than does burial, questions which are potentially problematic for contemporary Christian theology over the easy matching of burial and cremation. Pastorally too this equivalence has its problems over matters such as when the final parting is taken with the dead (Perham 1984:142). Where cremation has occurred in other cultures it has not had to play the role of preparing the dead for resurrection, even though it is associated with other ideas of salvation (Kearl 1989:180). In this chapter I explore these issues to stimulate discussion on what is a largely silent area of pastoral theology let alone of systematic theology.

THE SILENCE OF DEATH AS FAILURE

An interesting aspect of research on personal aspects of life is that people often say how much they have enjoyed talking about subjects which are seldom on public agendas. It seems as though a maturing takes place as individuals gain insight into their own vague yet long held views. The neutral and non-threatening attitude of a researcher often seems to foster this outcome.

This is true for some church people when it comes to the subject of death and the afterlife since these topics are amongst the least discussed in church or discussion groups. They are subjects hardly ever covered in religious education and many people of student age who have been interviewed say that they have hardly ever or never been formally introduced to the theme.

This silence is modern when compared with Victorian attitudes to death and the afterlife expressed both socially and in hymnody. It matches John Curl's (1972) wider cultural analysis of Victorians in their almost enthusiastic celebration of death contrasted with the twentieth century cloaking of mortality. Modern liturgy has for its part tended to stress the triumphant aspect of Christ's resurrection as experienced within the family and contemporary community. Personal success in life parallels this triumph of Christ and easily shifts the religious focus from a heavenly future of divine triumph to a contemporary sense of the achievement of God. At its worst this is interpreted as a religious power for successful achievements in business and family life, at its best it involves political theology and the desire to help the powerless attain power. Salvation is very much a present sense of success blessed by God. Traditionally the Protestant work ethic involved a sense of heavenly reward, there is much less of that element in contemporary British church life with the result that a future orientation within religious expectations seems generally less appropriate. In a success oriented culture death appears as a failure and lack of control. This kind of a move from future to present influences religious identity and has significant repercussions for cremation.

We begin with two Anglican Ministers giving diametrically opposite views on life after death in the Southwell survey of clergy.

1. 'I see both burial and cremation as a reverent disposal of a body. I always try to explain to the bereaved that it is but the outer shell of the loved one, whose soul and inner personality grow gradually towards God. They will meet again and be reunited in the place prepared for us all'.

2. 'There is so much nonsense written on this subject that I do not wish to add to it. It is not something about which we can have any sort of *knowledge*. It all depends on the sovereign action of God, and has nothing at all to do with the supposed continuation of the spirit or of the kind of soul which is seen as detachable from the body'.

These two portraits of belief express two distinctive outlooks on life which have, at times, been combined in the history of Christian doctrine (Chidester 1990:196).

Traditionally the burial of Christians in a grave made good symbolic sense in that the dead could await their resurrection at a future time just as Christ had awaited the divine act of the Father which had resulted in the resurrection.In early periods of the faith believers were buried in mass graves without personalized inscriptions, a situation totally unlike the personalized and individualized burials of the Victorian period (Brooks 1989), or the private placement of ashes in someone's garden in contemporary Britain. The collective burial of early Christians, preferably near the remains of a martyr, anticipated the communal resurrection of the last days. This doctrine of the resurrection was symbolically simple. Burial in a grave was consonant with scriptural accounts of the life of Christ and Christians could identify with the one they regard as their Saviour. The many parallels presented in the New Testament between Jesus and the believer reinforced this pattern of events which ordinary Christians could understand. As Jesus had been given a new and transformed existence so too would believers.

The history of theological ideas relating resurrection to the immortal soul is complex and embraces many cultural influences and philosophical debates (McManners 1981:148), and it may well be that the time is right for a more open consideration of these basic yet hard issues in the contemporary church where implicit and half formed ideas rule the day. It is all the more important because of the various beliefs of some other religions and their commitment to immortal life (Badham, P. and L. 1984).

The doctrine of the resurrection of the body has, for many Anglicans and for the broad Reformed tradition stressed the divine initiative as far as the future of individual persons is concerned. This has been very clearly expressed by, for example, William Temple in a particularly clear discussion of eternal life. 'Man is not immortal by nature or of right; but he is capable of immortality and there is offered to him resurrection from the dead and life eternal if he will receive it from God and on God's terms' (1935:472). Temple presses the point that authentic Christian doctrine of eternal life is not one of immortality but of resurrection. Resurrection is a gift of God and not 'an inherent right of the human soul' (1935:461). God alone is immortal in and of the divine nature. Temple wants a clear distinction between the Greek idea of immortal souls and the gift of resurrection which makes individuals immortal. Other, more recent, voices within the Church of England have argued that 'we ought to reject quite frankly the literalistic belief in a future resurrection of the actual physical frame which is laid in the tomb' (Richardson, 1987:274). This area is one where literalistic and metaphorical outlooks must inevitably engage with each other in attempting to grasp the substance of the Christian hope of everlasting life.

SOULS
It is this very issue of eternal soul versus God's gift of eternal life which stands at the theological cutting edge of pastoral theology and funeral practice and underlies the two positions of pastoral outlook cited above. If at death there is no eternal soul to pass on to some other realm the believer has to trust in God for an act of resurrection, itself a form of re-creation, if there is to be eternal life at all. In other words the doctrine of the resurrection is a doctrine of trust in God's capacity to continue and develop the individual as God wills it. The sense of hoping for the best is too vague and underplays the love of God as a motive for resurrection. Pastorally speaking these elements of trust and love stand to the fore in the belief in resurrection. They complement God's vindication of Christ as 'for us' and one of us. Belief in the Resurrection of Jesus in this sense completes belief the Incarnation. In a similar way, the hope of our own resurrection completes our own belief in Christ as 'God with us'.

Where a theology also gives place to immortal souls the scheme is somewhat different. Then an additional circuit is built into doctrine to account for what happens to that soul prior to its rejoining a resurrected body, or prior to its becoming the resurrected body. In general this integration of belief in immortal souls with resurrected bodies easily becomes philosophically complex and yet appeals to popular belief, (Rahner 1966.IV.351 ff).

The new Roman Catholic Order of Christian Funerals continues its traditional use of the journeying soul within its structure as first the Saints are asked to meet the soul, then Christ is asked to present it to God Most High. In the Prayer of Commendation it is the soul of the departed that is commended to God.

By contrast, in the funeral service approved in 1979 by the Archbishops of Canterbury and York for use in crematorium chapels the use of soul language is entirely avoided. During the committal the dead is 'entrusted' into God's hands and his or her body is committed to be cremated in the hope of resurrection to eternal life. The theological structure of the service is grounded in the burial-resurrection motif of Christ and therefore of the believer.

The Alternative Service Book of the Church of England itself avoids talk of the soul except insofar as the word occurs in psalms that are included for possible use. Within the service a distinction is made between commending and entrusting the dead to the mercy of God on the one hand, and the actual committal of the body to the ground or to be cremated on the other. It is quite likely that this dual procedure allows ample scope for people to read into the service ideas of the continuing soul.

CREMATION AND RESURRECTION

Cremation is a different process from burial in terms of human, natural, and technological involvements. Because of this cremation easily changes the pattern of traditional burial thought even though it often involves the burial of cremated remains.

In terms of what people say about their feelings the burial of ashes is not perceived in the same way as the burial of a body. Cremation triggers new thoughts about the future of the human self. The body is finished. This is the message of cremation. The ashes of cremation symbolize the fact of bodily dissolution rather than of the perpetuation of the deceased until some future day. In other words the ashes of cremation carry the opposite message from the remains of burial. The speed of the operation and the explicit technology involved make this evident to many people.

What cremation allows to come to the forefront is the otherwise strongly implicit belief in a human soul which leaves the body and continues into another dimension of existence at death. The traditional burial service focuses on the body and its resurrection future. While the modern cremation service explicitly follows that pattern its implicit message is that the body has come to its end but the soul has gone on. The only hope that many can read into the cremation service is the hope of a surviving soul. Even though it is sometimes argued that as far as God is concerned it is as easy to resurrect an individual from a myriad ashes as from a single grave this point carries little weight at the popular level of thought.

SCATTERING MEMORY

When people say they want their ashes scattered on the sea or on a favourite mountain walk their intention is not to give God an opportunity to show how easy it is to integrate and transform these bits and pieces into a heavenly body. Their intention is to express their association with these favoured places and to say something about their human interests while they lived. Special scattering is about the life already lived on earth and not about the life that is hoped to be lived beyond. In many respects the wishes to scatter ashes in places connected with the family,hobbies, or occupation indicates a form of continued association with these activities and places. The desire is to reinforce aspects of life on earth rather than direct attention to life in a world to come or beyond this mortality. In the song *The Joy of Living* the recent poet and musician Ewan MacColl expressed this sentiment very well:

> 'Take me to some high place
> Of heather, rock, and ling;
> Scatter my dust and ashes,
> Feed me to the wind.
> So that I will be
> Part of all you see,
> The air you are breathing . . .
> I'll be riding the gentle wind
> That blows through your hair;
> Reminding you how we shared
> In the joy of living'.

In this way for some people cremation fosters an association with past people and places, for others the belief that death is the final end, while for yet others it stresses the notion of an eternal soul. In probably also, at the same time, detracts from the traditional notion of resurrection. These two features of life-termination and the eternal soul are important aspects of cremation and both diverge from the traditional ideas of burial and resurrection. Some might argue that the burial of cremated remains overcomes the difference between burial and cremation and turns a cremation ultimately into a burial. But the burial of ashes does not seem to function in this way, serving more as a focus of the grief of the survivor and of a sense of identity or continued relationship with the dead than as the basis for a future resurrection for the deceased.

THE EMPTY TOMB, CREMATION, AND RESURRECTION LANGUAGE
In a strictly theological and abstract sense cremation offers a starker opportunity for the idea of resurrection to be clarified than does burial. Cremation renders the body to dust and thus back into its earthy base in a relative instant. The dissolution of the body in this way is the end-product of human life. Resurrection could equally well be re-creation, in the sense that unless God acts there is no hope at all for the person who once lived. There is no soul which can continue after death by its own right. In this way of looking at things trust in God is paramount.

The question of the dynamics of resurrection are necessarily vague. Practically no theological attention is now paid to the dust of death, to the atoms that once constituted a body and so on. Burial allowed all such questions to sink into the same grave of oblivion as the coffin. Since there was something in there somewhere that was sufficient to allow popular thought to assume that God would not have to 'start from scratch' on the last day. Since it is likely that most people who believed in such a resurrection of the body also believed in a soul that passed on it was true that all the eschatological eggs were not, in any case, in the same graveyard basket. Still the burial service focused on the body while the talk of eternity allowed free rein to the congregation's idea of the eternal soul.

Cremation is different. The body ends and offers very little symbolic scope for resurrection language. The vagueness of the grave becomes even vaguer and furnishes little basis for resurrection. In the absence of this opportunity the idea of the eternal soul comes to centre stage and, I suggest, does so in a dissonance with the burial language of the cremation service's approach to resurrection. Theologically speaking the language of resurrection, with its connotation of the divine initiative and grace in re-creating the believer, is denuded of its significance and is replaced by the notion of the eternal soul.

A more central theological issue behind the liturgical problem of cremation is the fact that Christ's resurrection is so directly related to the *motif* of the empty tomb. When theologians discuss interpretations of the resurrection, whether arguing the case for a literal resurrection of a transformed body or for a more symbolic interpretation, they still dwell upon the empty tomb.

It is precisely that empty tomb which is problematic for cremation symbolism. There is no doubt that the Christian theology of death is radically Christological. This means that a theology of cremation must also be Christological. The central theological truth of the resurrection is that God acted in relation to Jesus in such a way that Jesus becomes the focus of life for the rest of mankind. The meaning of life is focused on the resurrected Jesus, the source of vitality and the basis for understanding reality for mankind. Death, as the ground source of chaos and the flawedness of existence, is overcome and a new order of hope is inaugurated.

These truths of transformed life, meaning, and the overcoming of evil are capable of incorporating into a theology of cremation without liturgical play on the words of the empty tomb theme which include burial terms. But, and this is a more insupperable problem, death and resurrection motifs embraced by the empty tomb perspective are an intrinsic part of eucharistic practice, as they are of baptismal liturgies. Because of this it is inevitable that a degree of symbolic dissonance will occur between the complex of baptism, the passion, death, and resurrection of Christ, all Easter focused and eucharist related on the one hand, and cremation rites on the other. Since liturgy operates through an interplay of themes throughout church ritual and the church year a radically new form of ritual, such as cremation, cannot be integrated at a stroke.

INCREDULITY: RESURRECTION AND SOUL

But pastoral realism might also suggest that burial rites too do not simply flow in one natural stream that embraces the empty tomb language of the Bible and the faith of believers. Many at burials who read the liturgical language of the occasion in terms of eternal souls for, as we have showed, the majority of those who believe in life after death do not believe in the resurrection of the body.

In very practical terms the theological position which stresses a divine act of recreation in resurrection will not be appealing to many people because they will not understand it. In terms of stark realism there is some sense and intelligibility, however vague, in the idea of the soul leaving the body and going to God. To spell out the idea that at death the person dies and nothing happens to him or her until some future resurrection is to stretch the ordinary imagination to incredulity, even if some attempt is made to say that as far as the individual is concerned it would be just like falling asleep and waking up. Such a 'switching off' of a person until a future moment in eternity seems to make ideas of eternal life rather far fetched.

But this question is not simply one in which there is a clear church doctrine on which all are agreed. The responses of clergy on this topic varied to a tremendous extent. The two pictures outlined earlier in this chapter could be replicated many times. In general the emphasis seemed to fall more on the idea of the body being a physical entity while the real emphasis went on the soul. As one priest put it: 'In my understanding the funeral, whether burial or cremation, is merely the reverent disposal of the human body. The "soul" is still alive-resurrected'.

We mentioned at the outset of this book that cremation raises practical questions and makes theological demands which seminars in systematic theology can easily sidestep. The grammar of the soul offers one easy option but places the resurrection in a subsidiary position. Pastoral theology provokes systematic theology into deciding whether the doctrine of the resurrection is a supportive actor waiting in the wings or the great performer demanding centre stage.

6. Cremation as a Christian Ritual

Q. 'Who do you think should conduct the cremation service?'
A. 'Someone who can understand and try to ease any pain that those present may be feeling. Not in clerical double-talk but plain English'.

This fifty-year-old respondent had attended about a dozen cremations. He practises no religion and wants to be cremated. His reflections on a variety of themes bring us from statistics to one person whose views echo many present in crematoria chapels each week of the year. Here unbelief and faith interact in someone outside the church whose reflection is an incisive challenge to pastoral concern.

Here we give some of his answers when asked what he thought of the use of symbols in crematoria? Did he think crematoria were sacred places? Would he welcome a visit from a priest after a cremation service? What did he think of cremation services? Did he ever visit family graves? And what about any life after death?

'What are symbols for? The dead, surely not. It amazes me to think that religion becomes involved in this mumbo-jumbo. Christ was a carpenter. Did he need symbols, I think not. The "employees" who follow Jesus needed them as props and propaganda.

'If we are made in the image of God then we in some way must be holy: it follows everything we touch or inhabit then becomes holy.'

'I would welcome a visit from a priest while I am still here. But, seriously, what is a total stranger going to say? "Pity I never met your husband"?'

'No vicar ever seems to know the guy in the box.'

'Occasionally I visit my granny's grave. I like to walk around graveyards and think of the people there, once like us, laughing, crying, having families, rows, tragedies. It makes me realize I am not as clever as sometimes I think I am, nor as unique.'

'If we don't continue after death albeit in a different form what has all this been about? Sometimes I don't believe in anything—the rottenness of things pisses me off, and then I look at my children and my garden and I know the "MAN" is still involved with us.'

CREMATION SERVICES: SOME POPULAR VIEWS

From this personal cameo we return to the statistical overview presented by the Nottinghamshire survey of 459 people, and in-depth interviews with 62 individuals. Those interviewed personally were asked to select one cremation they had attended as the focus for their answers. In what follows we condense much material into a flowing description of cremation rather than dealing extensively with each topic.

Of the 459 respondents only 10% had not attended a cremation compared with 20% who had not attended a burial. This emphasizes the normative status cremation has actually achieved in Britain. In all 46% had been to between two and five cremations, while 26% had been to between six and fifteen. Along with surveys of students which I have conducted a slight majority tended to underestimate the percentage of people cremated in Britain each year, which indicates the lag that exists between social reality and cultural images.

More tended to think of crematoria as sacred places (52%) than as not being sacred (37%). Only a small minority (7%) thought that the religious symbols present in most crematoria were inappropriate; 31% thought them quite appropriate but the majority had no opinion.

Some 70% thought that the cremation services they had attended had, by and large, been pleasing. Less than 1% thought there was too much religion involved, and only 9% referred to a sense of being rushed in too short a time. This figure is interesting given the widespread conversational comment about the speed of the ceremony, but when asked how they would improve the ceremony only 7% asked for more time. But 4% thought that less religion should be included in new services, a figure relating to our discussion elsewhere in this book on the issue of non-religious services and perhaps hints at a general contentment with a religious perspective even though people other than clergy might conduct the proceedings. The fact that the priest was an unknown individual was mentioned by 7% of respondents. As far as the appearance of crematoria was concerned 62% had no view while, practically speaking, as many thought their architecture good (14%) as thought it bad (12%). Some 60% thought crematorium gardens were generally good.

SENSE OF REALITY, TIME, AND MUSIC

Moving to the more detailed, and more personal issues, of those who were interviewed we found that the great majority (81%) thought that services were well conducted with only 7% being badly led. Yet alongside this acceptance lay the interesting fact of the sense of reality conferred by it. A majority of individuals (58%) said the service did feel real to them, but 23% said it felt unreal while another 5% reckoned they felt like a spectator. There are many issues involved here, both in terms of degree of relation to the deceased, and the psychological state of individuals. Only 15% had no opinion on this reality factor. The same percentage also had no recollection whether there was music or not at the cremation, this contrasts with the 34% who remember live organ music and 48% who thought the music was taped. By and large music seems to provide a useful dimension to the event since 65% thought they benefited from having had music while only 16% thought it had detracted from the service, normally because it was taped and appeared too artificial.

As to duration those interviewed reflected the broader population survey with just over 9% thinking the service had been too short. Some 5% thought it too long, but 60% thought the timing was just right. An additional 8% viewed the time as adequate because there had been a prior service in church: 17% were unsure over the time factor.

COFFIN, AND EMOTIONAL TRIGGERS

No one who was interviewed thought that cremation was a more emotional occasion than burial. In fact 57% thought that burial was more emotional but 43% thought there was no difference.

In the surveys at least there seems to be very little evidence to suggest that burial is perceived as more therapeutic than cremation, though this point is very often argued and has almost attained the status of a psychological truth in some quarters.It is important that pastors should not accept ideas of particular social groups on matters of emotion, mood, and personality as being universally applicable. In a society where some psychological notions assume the status of assured certainty caution is meritorious. This is not to say that in a very few specific cases of, for example, tragic and sudden death of a younger life the option between burial and cremation does not matter. In some such cases burial is the safest option since it does not give occasion for regret in having 'destroyed' what had already been 'killed'. A traditional grave can be helpful in such cases of accident and sudden death, though there is a potential problem of morbid pre-occupation with the grave of someone to whom the survivor remains strongly attached. These specific cases need emphasizing since they are easily lost in a welter of population statistics.

Perhaps the fact that 86% of respondents did not think that cremation affected the memory of a dead person any more than did burial might be a useful hint to the role of funerals within the adaptability of people. Only 7% thought that the memory of their dead had been reduced in significance through cremation.

As far as the cremation service is concerned most people seem to remember what happened at them. The great majority recall what happened to the coffin as far as its mode of exit or separation is concerned. As to the actual location of the coffin within the chapel area the majority (71%) felt that it was about right in relation to the congregation.Just about 5% felt it was too far away and as many (5%) felt it was too close. The sense of the coffin being too far away was especially important in the case of the death of small children when the diminutive size of the coffin standing in its allocated place gave a sense of loneliness. An issue close to that of isolation touches the relative inactivity of people in relation to the coffin of adults.

To explore this theme people were asked in the interviews if they thought it a good idea that the congregation might gather round or near to the coffin for the committal. This would help bring the departing individual into social focus since it sometimes seems as though the dead person is marginal to the service: an additional feature to a service aimed at the living. Some 32% of people thought such a gathering useful but exactly 50% did not think so: 18% were undecided. One feature that attracted no support whatsoever was the question of having the coffin open at some stage in the cremation ceremony (95% no, 5% unsure).

RITUAL SHAPE OF CREMATION

Fulfilling the title of this book *Cremation Today and Tomorrow* we now move from surveys of the contemporary situation to the structure of funeral rites and then to an example enshrining some of these ideas.

The anthropological idea of rites of passage has now gained wide, and some-times uncritical, acceptance amongst church leaders. Like the sociological idea of charisma it has become part of general vocabulary, but like that idea it needs to be used carefully. In rites of passage individuals pass from one social status to another and are helped to do so by society. Rites of passage involve both individuals and groups, in that individuals are not left to their own devices but are taken in hand by society and led through the changes of status that befall them.

In classical anthropological theory this ritual change is always spoken of in the plural, rites of passage, rather than a single rite of passage. One reason for this is because Arnold Van Gennep, the originator of the idea, believed that any ritual of transition involved three processes, (1960). These three rites of passage constitute the total process of status change and change in position in society; they are the rites of (i) separation, (ii) transition, and (iii) reincorporation. The individual is thus separated from the initial status, enters a period of transition which is usually marginal to the full stream of social life, and finally is reincorporated into society by virtue of the newly gained identity. Van Gennep also called these stages the pre-liminal, liminal, and post-liminal stages following the Latin notion of *limen* as threshold.

Within the whole process of rites of passage it is usual for several categories of people to undergo a change of status in relation to each other. In weddings for example not only do the bride and groom each gain a spouse, but their parents gain additional in-law children, and also experience new forged links with the other parents. Friends of the bride and groom also change their relationship as their single friend becomes a married person. In very many rituals of social status change this kind of complex shift in mutual relationships and identities occurs.

As far as cremation rites are concerned the work of the anthropologist Robert Hertz is at least as important as that of Van Gennep on rites of passage (Huntingdon and Metcalf 1979). Hertz focused on funerary rites involving a double ritual, the first part dealing with the corruptible flesh which he saw as the wet symbolic medium of the body; and the second dealing with the bones or skeleton, the dry medium of the body. The first phase whether it involved interment or cremation was,he thought, a time for the bones to dry whether slowly through the decay of the flesh or rapidly through fire. So it is that he describes cremation.

'This is precisely the meaning of cremation: far from destroying the body of the deceased, it recreates it and makes it capable of entering into new life' (1960:43).

If there is any truth in Hertz's observation, despite the fact that his argument was grounded in the behaviour of non-Christian cultures, then it has been completely ignored in analyses of Christian cremation rites. In this book we have at least raised the issue for discussion.

But whether in the double ritual of cremation and of placing ashes, or in the direct burial of a body, rites of passage occur. In many traditional societies the dead pass into the domain of the ancestors where they have distinctive roles to play towards their living descendants (Chidester 1990:34). In modern British society there must, inevitably, be a very complex view of the destiny of the dead depending upon the beliefs of the deceased and also of the living survivors. As we have seen, it is likely that for half the population the dead simply come to the end of all existence, except as a memory and as part of the identity of the survivors. But this identity-constitutive element is not unimportant, it is fundamentally significant as that aspect of the rite of passage which deals with the living.

Certainly from the theological standpoint this emphasis on the living should not be allowed to predominate. The funeral rite as such is not primarily a therapeutic ritual for the living, it is the means by which the dead individual is publically acknowledged as now belonging to another order of existence. The former life with its status and story may be rehearsed as a means of emphasizing its termination. A new phase in relation to God through Christ must be formally initiated. As the dead individual is thus located by the Christian community and by the natural family the survivors too are relocated themselves. Here then we have the two major foci of the cremation rite: a rite of passage for the dead and a rite of passage for the living as relationships now alter. But the processes involved in burial can differ markedly from those of cremation as the following scheme displays in possible post-liminal paths:

Pre-liminal	Sickness, Hospitalization, Death		
Liminal	Undertakers Duties, Post-Mortem, Chapel of Rest or Funeral 'Home' Journey to Crematorium or Graveyard		
Post-liminal	Funeral Service: Paths		
	One	Two	Three
Phase 1	Body—Buried	Ashes—Received	Ashes—Received
Phase 2	—	Ashes—Buried	Ashes—Special place

The key issues centre in the post-liminal period which I have divided into two phases. Burial normally ends with phase one when the body is buried and that is the end of the human remains as far as the living are concerned. Grief and memory may be related to visits to the grave but the deceased has been finally located on the day of burial.

With cremation there is a second phase to the post-liminal period. This is a new phenomenon as far as modern British funerals are concerned and results in ambiguity, and confusion for some people. Many jokes about ashes express this confusion as humour so often does in areas of embarrassment and uncertainty. The ashes that follow Path Two differ from those of Path Three.

Path Two ashes are buried in graves, often of other family members, and by a religious service. The Alternative Service Book has provided a short rite to deal with this eventuality though as I have already indicated it involves a repetition of committal and implies a previous passage of the deceased into God's care.

Path Three ashes may go in a number of directions. They may resemble the Path Two remains by being placed either in the earth or on the earth at a crematorium area of remembrance. But, more significantly, they may be taken away by the relatives and undergo any number of treatments, some examples of which have already been given. The significance of this sort of Path Three activity is twofold. On the one hand it speaks of the private identity of the dead, and on the other it marks a 'this-worldly' destiny for the dead. When a person's ashes are placed on a rose bed or on a cricket field it emphasizes and in a sense fulfils that individuals' life: where your identity is there will your ashes be also.

In terms of Christian theology such privatizing and this-worldly focusing of the identity of the dead is unacceptable. Pastorally it must be remembered that cremation has opened a possibility that never existed before in allowing the physical symbol of identity, the ashes, to be in private hands. In one sense this is the final expression of a culture of privacy and individualism.How different this is from the public monuments of recent centuries (Rahtz 1981:117). The eschatological framework of the Christian faith is transformed into potentially idiosyncratic decisions of private individuals. At that point it becomes impossible to speak of social rites of passage.

LITURGICAL AND PASTORAL CONSEQUENCES
It is because the actual cremation service has been identified with the burial service that the disposal of the ashes has assumed a secondary place. It is assumed that the cremation service will be a standard form and the treatment of the ashes will be an optional extra, dependent upon the religious belief, wishes, or whims, of the kin.

Liturgically and pastorally speaking it would make better sense to know the final destination of the ashes before the form of the actual cremation service is decided upon. In an ideal world the cremation process should be established according to the two phased pattern of the postliminal period. In practical terms this is not easy and it is likely to be the case that a disjunction will often occur between cremation service and final placement of ashes. At least these are issues which pastors need to have clearly in mind. It is likely that those who disbelieve in an afterlife will increasingly make use of Path Three in the Post-liminal period, and it is quite possible that they will avail them-selves of a service that reflects more upon the life-lived than upon the life to come. The part traditionally played by the doctrine of the resurrection in such contexts will be replaced by a memorial location special to the deceased. Fulfilment belongs to the past and to being at one with things or places that meant much in life. Resurrection beliefs will have a future and a more open dimension to them.

It is with such thoughts in mind that we now conclude by furnishing a sample Cremation Service followed by a Service for placement of the Ashes. Both seek to express Christologically focused doctrine grounded in the idea of resurrection as re-creation and not dependent upon the notion of an eternal soul.

The suggested form of services below seeks to distinguish between moments when the ritual addresses changes in the status of dead and of the living. It would be possible to make the form of service far more comprehensive in terms of options but this level of simplicity will help focus reader's attention on critical issues. There are some very useful additional forms of intercession and thanksgiving provided in *Patterns for Worship*, a Report by the Liturgical Commission of the General Synod of the Church of England, (1989:145,160, 183,199,211,222). But the Commission did not offer any unified and specific material on cremation as a specific form of service. This perhaps is where our final chapter may be useful in stimulating criticism and creative liturgy.

7. Services

Service of Cremation

1 *Minister:*

Christ being raised from the dead dies no more,
Death has no more dominion over him.
In dying he died to sin once for all,
In living he lives to God.
For as in Adam all die,
Even so in Christ shall all be made alive.

1a *Minister may say:*

Alleluia Christ is risen.

All: **He is risen indeed. Alleluia.**

2 *The congregation is welcomed or greeted in an appropriate way and is asked to sit as the Minister addresses them thus OR begins with 3 OR 4:*

2a *Minister may say*

Our Christian hope is in the power of God.
In the power of Creation that makes the world,
In the lowly power of Redemption that saves the world,

In the image of God we were made,
In the image of Christ we will be refashioned.
God's steadfast promise brought Jesus through death to
Be the source of all life,
In that life we trust.

Of ourselves we have no right to eternity,
No life of our own to last forever,
This is our weakness and our loss,
The cause of our grief.

Let us then turn to God who is rich in mercy,
And who will not leave us abandoned.

3 *A Hymn may be sung.*

4 *Minister says the words of:*

Our Life and Hope

In our loss O Lord we seek your presence
In our uncertainty your love.

You are nearer to us than we know,
In you we have our being,
As we live, we live in you,
As we die, we die in you.

From dust you made us and dust we are,
Yours alone is the power of our living breath.
You are our Maker and Redeemer,
Our Lord of Life and hope,
In you alone we trust.

5   *The Minister continues:*
    As family and friends we gather,as part of God's great family of grace we
    pray as Christ taught us saying together:

    Our Father who art in heaven . . .
    For ever, and ever, Amen.

6   Now hear the word of God in Holy Scripture:
    (A friend, family member, or Minister reads:)

7   *A Hymn may be sung here*

8   *Recalling the Past Life of the Dead.*
    The Minister says:
    And now O Lord we remember (Name) your servant
    Recalling times spent together
    And giving thanks for his (her) life,
    For joys and trials shared,
    For work accomplished,
    For leisure, for family life, and friendship.

    *(Particular relationships may be mentioned and any address or reflection be
    delivered now.)*

    The Minister continues:

    In silence we share the memories of our hearts.

9   *Silence*

10 *The Minister says:*
    And now O Lord we pray for ourselves
    As we part from the body of this our brother (sister).
    As we needed grace in life together
    Now grant us grace for life apart.

11 *The Minister says:*
    Let us stand to make our parting.

    *(The Minister, family member, friend, or attendant may light a large candle (Eas-
    ter Candle) set beside the coffin on which a flower may be placed and around which
    the congregation may be invited to gather, before the Minister says the Prayer of
    Light during which the Committal takes place)*

12 *Prayer of Light*
O Lord by whose word the heavens were made,
Whose love made us from dust,
Receive now the mortal remains of this your servant
Departed this earthly life.

Dutifully we give his (her) body for cremation,
As ashes to ashes and dust to dust,
In the hope of life eternal,
Through Christ our Risen Lord.

(During these last words the coffin is removed and the Minister continues with minimum pause)
That as the flames of earth end our mortality
So in the fulness of time the flame of your love
May remake us eternally in the
Glory and stature of Christ,

He alone is the Light of the world,
The light no darkness can end,
Who with you and the Holy Spirit,
Is God for ever and ever,
Amen.

13 *A Hymn may be sung and people return to their seats.*

14 *The candle is extinguished by an appropriate person.*

15 *EITHER the Minister says:*
Having committed the future of our brother (sister)
To God in Christ,
Let us resolve to live wisely
In the time now given us
Through the strength that comes from God.

15a *OR the Minister says:*
The eternal future of our brother (sister)
Is in the hands of God in Christ.
As we have prayed for him (her) in the fellowship
Of all believers, that great Communion of Saints,
So let us pray for ourselves,
Firmly resolving to live wisely in the days ahead,
By the strength that comes from God.

16 *The Minister says:*
The Spirit of love in the light of Christ
Unite us in that one fellowship of trust
And bring us all to his eternal kingdom.

And the peace of God which passes all understanding
Keep your hearts and minds in the knowledge and love of God
and of his Son Jesus Christ our Lord,
and the blessing of God Almighty
the Father, the Son, and the Holy Spirit,
be with us all evermore. Amen.

*　　*　　*

44 *Cremation Today and Tomorrow*

Post-Cremation Service

1   *The Minister addresses those present:*
     The Lord God of creation
     Who made the heavens and the earth
     Also made us from the dust of the ground.
     God it is who gives us the breath of life,
     The gift of thought, and the joy of living.
     And when our days are ended,
     And our mortality known,
     Then are we returned to the ground,
     For out of it were we taken,
     And to it we return.

2   *The Remains are buried or otherwise placed.*
     (A family member may throw earth onto the grave or amidst the remains at the
     appropriate time).

     The Minister says:
     As fellow creatures and members of the family of God
     we committed our brother's (sister's) body for cremation,
     now we fulfil our duty by returning his (her) earthly remains to the
     ground,
     As earth to earth, ashes to ashes, and dust to dust,
     Through Jesus Christ our Lord.
     Amen.

3   Let us pray.
     You alone O Lord God are the source of life eternal,
     You our comfort, hope, and strength.
     We have no power of ourselves to help ourselves,
     No right to immortality.
     To you then O Lord we look for newness of life
     Both now in the days of our mortal flesh,
     And finally, by the gift of resurrection,
     In your eternal kingdom.
     You who are One God now and forever. Amen.

4   The grace of our Lord Jesus Christ, and the love of God, and the
     fellowship of the Holy Spirit be with us all evermore. Amen.